Groovy Gravity

by Rena Korb

illustrations by Brandon Reibeling

Content Consultant:
Paul Ohmann, Ph.D. • Associate Professor of Physics • University of St. Thomas

visit us at www.abdopublishing.com

Printed in the United States.

Text by Rena Korb
Illustrations by Brandon Reibeling
Edited by Nadia Higgins
Interior layout and design by Ryan Haugen
Cover design by Brandon Reibeling

Library of Congress Cataloging-in-Publication Data

Korb, Rena B.
  Groovy gravity / Rena Korb ; illustrated by Brandon Reibeling ; content consultant, Paul Ohmann.
    p. cm. — (Science rocks!)
  ISBN 978-1-60270-039-0
  1. Gravitation—Juvenile literature. 2. Gravity—Juvenile literature. I. Reibeling, Brandon, ill. II. Title.
  QC178.K835 2008
  531'.14—dc22
                        2007006324

Table of Contents

A Powerful Force

Stand outside and look around. The ground lies beneath your feet. The sky stretches above your head.

You are standing on Earth. Our planet is like a giant ball floating in space.

Now think about kids standing on the other side of Earth. The ground lies beneath their feet. The sky stretches above their heads.

How can that be? What keeps these kids from falling off Earth?

A force called gravity pulls the kids toward the ground.
It keeps them from flying into space.

Gravity works on everybody and everything. You can't see gravity, but it is a basic part of nature.

Scientists only learned about gravity a few hundred years ago.
But it has been around since time began.

How Gravity Works

Gravity is a powerful force of attraction. It tries to pull two things together.

Look around your room. Every object in it is affected by gravity. Your pencils, shoes, books, clothes, and bed are pulling at each other. So why aren't your pencil and eraser flying across your desk to meet?

Small objects, such as pencils, erasers, and ants, have a very weak pull of gravity. Large objects pull much more strongly. The heavier an object, the harder it will pull.

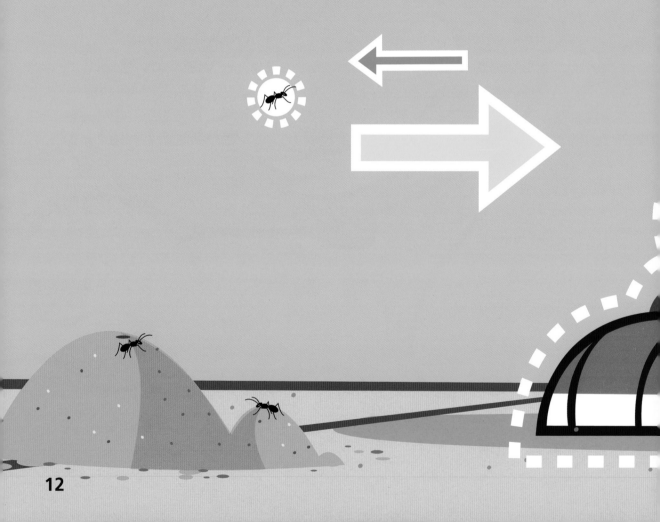

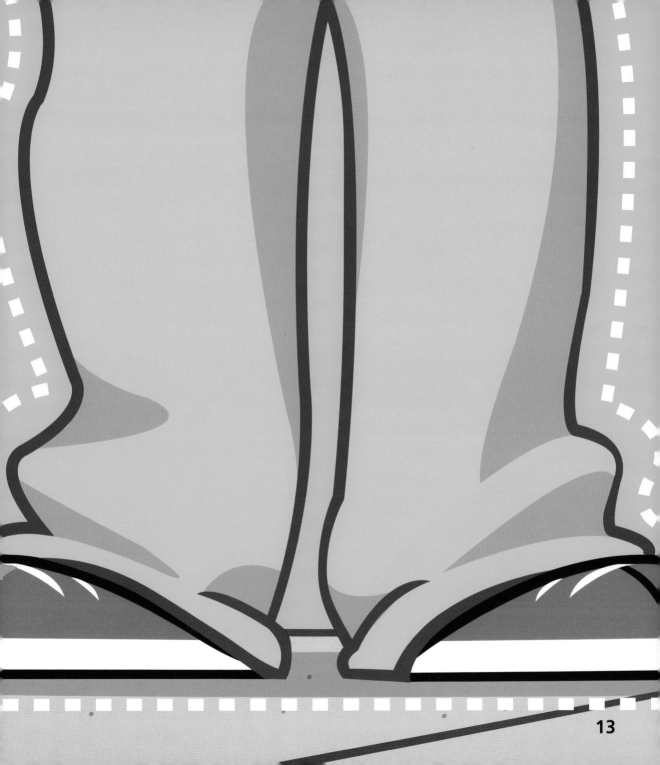

Earth's Gravity

Earth is bigger than the houses, trees, people and everything else on it.
Earth's gravity is strong enough to keep your home sitting on the ground. It is strong enough to keep the tree you like to climb from drifting away.

The force of gravity is a little stronger at the North Pole than it is around Earth's equator.

Jump up! Earth's gravity quickly pulls you down. Throw a ball, and it falls down.

Imagine going down a slide with no gravity.
You wouldn't slide down at all!

Gravity also makes rain fall to the ground. It makes leaves drift down from trees.

Gravity in Space

Gravity also works in outer space. Planets, moons, and stars pull on each other.

Smaller objects often orbit, or travel around, bigger objects. Earth orbits the sun. The moon orbits Earth. Gravity keeps everything in place.

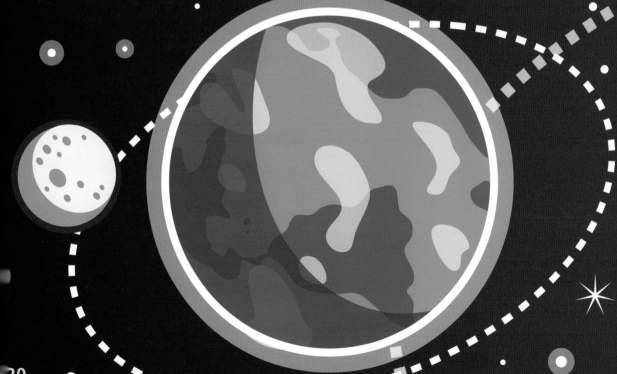

Without gravity, the moon would be gone from the night's sky. It would have shot away into space.

Earth's gravity is stronger than the moon's. So if Earth is pulling on the moon, why doesn't the moon come crashing down?

The moon never stops speeding around Earth. The moon's speed keeps it from crashing into our planet.

Use a yo-yo to see how the moon stays up. Spin the yo-yo in a circle around you. The yo-yo only drops when it stops moving.

Perfect Gravity

Jump. Skip. Kick a ball! Earth's gravity is just the right strength for your body.

If you lived on a planet as big as Jupiter, it would be hard to even lift your foot from the ground!

If you lived on the moon, you'd float a little with each step.

Activity

How Fast Does It Fall?

In the 1600s, the scientist Galileo took two balls to the top of a tower in Italy. One ball weighed more than the other. Most people thought the heavier ball would hit the ground first. But the balls landed at the same time! Galileo had shown that gravity makes objects fall at the same speed. You can see this for yourself.

What you need:

Newspaper

A ball

A paperclip

What to do:

1. Spread several sheets of newspaper at your feet.
2. Hold the ball in one hand and the paperclip in the other. Make sure to hold both objects at the same height.
3. Open both hands at one time, letting the two objects fall.
4. Listen for when the objects hit the ground. You can hear how they land on the newspaper at the same time.

Fun Facts

Gravity makes falling objects gather speed. Objects fall faster as they zoom closer to the ground.

An English scientist named Isaac Newton explained how gravity worked during the 1600s. He saw an apple fall from a tree. He wondered why apples always fell toward the ground and never sideways or upward. Soon, he had figured out that the apples were being pulled toward Earth by gravity.

Your weight is a measure of how hard gravity is pulling you toward the ground. If you weigh 50 pounds (23 kilograms) on Earth, you'd weigh 118 pounds (54 kilograms) on Jupiter and only about 8 pounds (4 kilograms) on the moon.

Glossary

attraction—a force pulling two objects toward each other.

equator—an imaginary line that circles around the middle of Earth.

force—a push or pull that causes an object to change its speed or the direction it is moving.

gravity—the force that pulls a smaller object toward a larger object.

object—a thing you can see or touch.

orbit—the movement of one space object traveling around another, such as the moon orbiting Earth.

On the Web

To learn more about gravity, visit ABDO Publishing Company on the World Wide Web at **www.abdopublishing.com**. Web sites about gravity are featured on our Book Links page. These links are routinely monitored and updated to provide the most current information available.

Index